CAMINO MEDITATIONS

30

*Mindful Walking Meditations to
Conquer Addiction and Cultivate Joy*

KELLY WATT

Library of Congress Cataloging-in-Publication Data
Watt, Kelly, author.
Camino Meditations: Mindful Walking Meditations for
Conquering Addiction and Cultivating Joy/by Kelly Watt.
pages cm
ISBN 978-0-9836668-2-0 (alk.paper)
1. Buddhist meditations.
2. Walking—Religious aspects—Buddhism.
3. Camino de Santiago. 1. Title.
BQ5580.W38 2014
294.3'4435—dc23

2014002423

Hamilton Stone Editions
Maplewood, New Jersey

Cover and Interior Formatting by
KUHN Design Group | kuhndesigngroup.com

Other Books by Kelly Watt:

Mad Dog

For all seekers everywhere
who wander their way to the Infinite.

CONTENTS

Introduction 13

The Guidelines 19

The Serenity Prayer 21

Traditional Buddhist Scripture 23

Camino Prep 25

Day One: Es Su Camino 28

Day Two: *Siga Las Flechas* or Follow the Arrows 30

Day Three: Follow the *Eros* *32*

Day Four: Be Kind To Your Feet 34

Day Five: Honour Your Own Rhythm 36

Day Six: Carry Only What You Need 38

Day Seven: What Does Your Seigneur (or Source)
Have to Say To You? 40

Day Eight: The Bigger the Mountain, the Smaller the Steps . . . 42

Day Nine: Gratitude is the Greatest of Virtues 44

Day Ten: *Thinking Is Free, Breathing is Free, God is Free* *46*

Day Eleven: The Camino Provides 48

Day Twelve: *Une Revision de Vie* or Review Your Life 50

Day Thirteen: Wash Your Socks 52

Day Fourteen: Spiritual Friends 54

Day Fifteen: Sharing 56

DAY SIXTEEN: In God's Time 58

DAY SEVENTEEN: *The Heart Has No Wrinkles, Only Scars* *60*

DAY EIGHTEEN: Your Happy Talisman 62

DAY NINETEEN: When It Rains the Pack is Less Heavy! 64

DAY TWENTY: How You Walk the Camino,
is How You Are in Life 66

DAY TWENTY-ONE: In the End It's All About Your Stuff 68

DAY TWENTY-TWO: The Ghosts of Pilgrims Past 70

DAY TWENTY-THREE: A Good Place to Die 72

DAY TWENTY-FOUR: Detach with Love 74

DAY TWENTY-FIVE: You Are Not Your Thoughts 76

DAY TWENTY-SIX: God (Source) Has Already Forgiven You . . . 78

DAY TWENTY-SEVEN: Keep Walking 80

DAY TWENTY-EIGHT: The Camino Is Going to Santiago,
Where Are You Going? 82

DAY TWENTY-NINE: Once a Pilgrim, Always a Pilgrim 84

DAY THIRTY: Kissing Samadhi 86

DAY THIRTY-ONE: The Lessons of the Pilgrim 88

DAY THIRTY-TWO: Joy @ the End of the World 90

EPILOGUE: The End is Only The Beginning 92

Acknowledgements 95

About the Author 97

But not only does the goal of the pilgrimage lend a new significance to the present and the future; it also lights up the past. It makes every idlest step of worth. It makes us so understanding of the past that we would not alter one jot or tittle in it. Our whole life is transfigured.

STEPHEN GRAHAM, *Tramp's Sketches (1912)*

CAMINO MEDITATIONS

INTRODUCTION

H ippocrates said, "Walking is man's best medicine." When
my life was in disarray, I took him literally. In June 2008,
I flew to Bilbao and began walking, and I continued walking for seven weeks.

When I tell people that I walked the Camino de Santiago,
the 800-kilometre pilgrimage route through northern Spain,
they often ask me: Why did you walk all that way? I have a short
answer and a long answer to that question. The short answer is: I
had turned fifty and wanted to do something memorable. But the
long answer is more complicated. The truth is, I walked because
I was grieving: I suspected I could no longer have children of
my own; my career was in a shambles; I was a child sexual abuse
survivor who still suffered from post-traumatic stress symptoms
despite years of therapy and numerous attempts to find resolu-
tion. I was cross-addicted: I had an eating disorder and drank
heavily. I realized I would never heal my food addiction without letting go of alcohol first. I drank to feel brave, but inevitably woke up feeling ashamed and more afraid. So, I decided to
commit to a trial abstinence while walking the Camino, using
The Way as an ambulatory rehab, a movable retreat.

Most pilgrims who walk the route known as the Camino
Frances, begin in St. Jean Pied-de-Port in France, continue

through Basque country to Santiago, the purported resting place of the bones of the Apostle St. James. But I decided to skip the arduous slog up the Pyrenees and began in Pamplona, Spain. I walked to Santiago then decided to continue on to Finisterre on the Atlantic Ocean. Once known as *Fins Terre* or the end of the world in French, it was the final destination for the Celts who originated this pilgrimage hundreds of years ago.

I began by walking in silence every morning, during that time I meditated and prayed. I had learned to meditate in Nepal when I was 18 years old. After graduating from missionary high school in India, I ended out in a Tibetan Buddhist monastery called Kopan. For 30 days I sat cross-legged in a canvas tent listening to discourses from a charming, wise, and funny Tibetan Lama about the inevitability of my death and the great good fortune of my human rebirth. Lama Yeshe taught us the importance of sitting peacefully in silence, breathing, and getting to know our thoughts. During the thirty-day retreat we weren't allowed to lie, steal, wear perfume or jewellery, watch movies, listen to radios, write letters, or contact the outside world. A western monk explained to me that if I practiced these principles and meditated for one entire moon cycle, my mind would never be the same. He was right.

Meditation changed my life, as clichéd as that sounds. It's hard to believe this now but in 1977 it wasn't a very cool thing to do. Now scientists study meditation to prove what yogis have known all along: That mindfulness practices can potentially heal the body, speech, and mind; and create new neural pathways in brains traumatized by violence and war. But the thing I noticed most when starting to sit on a cushion at 18, was that meditation changed my relationship with myself. For the first time in my life, I sat down and made friends with my thoughts, became aware of my own inner dialogue. It was revelatory to learn that my outer world had a way of replicating my inner thoughts. That the best way to change my life, was to change myself, starting with my thoughts.

I have my dog Hannah to thank for teaching me to combine walking *with* meditation. I used to struggle every morning with whether to meditate first thing or take my feisty wheaten terrier for walkies. My life in those days was incredibly sedentary. I sat all day at a computer, writing, so by the end of the day I was loathe to sit for another 30 minutes. I wondered what would happen if I combined walking with meditating, and not slow-mo meditative walking, but real walk the dog walking. Wouldn't that manage to wake up the body while purifying the mind? I hoped it would bring my practice out of my reclusive meditation room, (in reality my green chair) and out into the ordinary world, as Lama Yeshe had encouraged.

I should confess here that I'm a Hi-Bu. A Buddhist with a Higher Power. I'd found solace in Twelve Step Recovery, Life Coaching, Psychotherapy *and* Buddhism and I wanted to combine elements of these different traditions. So, I brought my practices with me to Spain. For seven weeks, I prayed, meditated, wrote to a spiritual friend, answered the life questions she sent me, abstained from alcohol, and walked for roughly 20 kilometers a day.

I did Vajrasattva, a Tibetan Buddhist purification practice using white light. I'd been doing this cleansing visualization and mantra with a group of Buddhist friends for over twenty-five years. When I was finished in the mornings, I walked in silence watching my breath. I noticed without fail that at the end of every morning, no matter how miserable I felt at the start of each day, by the end of two to three hours of praying, meditating, and walking, I felt better. Strangely joyous. Happy in the middle of howling wind and rain. Go figure.

The more I walked, meditated, and contemplated my life, the more I realized that anyone could do what I was doing. We live in a time where many healing resources are available: Mindfulness, EFT, somatic therapy, life coaching, and recovery programs for people suffering from every manner of compulsion. Committing to practices on three levels—the physical, emotional, and spiritual—accelerates healing. I believe anyone can combine Western tools with Eastern meditation techniques and experience a profound spiritual shift.

By the end of the trek, I decided to simplify these practices so that people of all spiritual persuasions could use them to overcome shame and grief, loss and addiction, and cultivate happiness. The average pilgrim takes 30 to 35 days to walk the Camino, so I've included 33 chapters with meditations, journal questions and action steps. These are coupled with Camino slogans I learned along the way. I chose approximately 30 days because meditation masters and behavioural scientists alike know that 30 is a magical number. If you practice any new habit for a month, it becomes ingrained. If you happen to take longer than 30 days to walk your personal pilgrimage, take more rest days, allow yourself several days for one lesson, or revisit the ones you find particularly useful. To include people of all faiths, I have used the terms, *Higher Power,* and *Source* for God.

Whether you're going on a month-long pilgrimage or simply walking the dog around the block every morning while watching your thoughts, as you venture outward, you will also journey within. What follows is, I hope, a simple workbook to use on one's spiritual adventure. These meditations are designed for walkers, but can be done sitting down on a bench, lying in bed, anywhere you choose to investigate the labyrinth of your own mind.

For there comes a day when we all need to go on a sacred journey. As the Buddha said: *Life is suffering.* If we live long enough, we will lose someone we love, watch a dream die, succumb to weakness, folly, misadventure, poverty, illness and finally death. But when disaster strikes, we can cope with dignity if we practice mindfulness and have tools for connecting with our Spiritual Source. In both recovery and Mahayana Buddhism, it is said, that to keep your spiritual growth you must pass it on to someone else. May these mindful walking practices free you of grief and shame, addiction, and all manner of suffering. May they fill you with the Sunlight of the Spirit. May they leave you happy, joyous, and ultimately free.

THE GUIDELINES

1. Walk at your own pace.

2. Walk in silence in the mornings.

3. Meditate and pray every day.

4. Journal once a day.

5. Follow your joy (but notice when you're following your pain!)

6. Avoid alcohol and drugs for 30 days.

7. Take occasional duvet or rest days.

THE SERENITY PRAYER

God grant me the serenity,
to accept the things I cannot change,
the courage to change the things I can,
and the wisdom to know the difference.

TRADITIONAL
BUDDHIST SCRIPTURE

What is born will die,
What has been gathered will be dispersed,
What has been accumulated will be exhausted,
What has been built up will collapse,
And what has been high will be brought low.

THE BUDDHA

CAMINO PREP

People often want to know how to prepare for a pilgrimage. The answer is simple: Start walking. I walked gradually increasing the length and time for approximately six weeks before departure. This gave me an opportunity to develop strength as well as try out my boots, my socks, my walking stick and hat. (Boots are your most important purchase: They must be *uber* comfortable and broken in, although beyond that it's personal choice.) After a month I began carrying my knapsack and gradually added weight. This last is the most important thing. I added small five-pound weights to my pack until I'd reached my approximate carrying weight. You don't need to walk 20 kilometers a day to prepare, you can build up to that length on the Camino or your preferred pilgrimage route itself. Of course, that's harder to do if you decide to begin by scaling the Pyrenees. Whatever you do, do it gradually to prevent injury.

There is one cardinal rule to packing for the Camino and everyone breaks it: Travel light! It is 778-kilometres to Santiago, that is roughly 1,500,000 steps, so, you don't want to be carrying a small refrigerator on your back. Ten percent of your body weight is one suggestion or under 10 kg. The less you carry the less likely you are to be injured, and the easier your trip. Trust me, you need very little. There are light-weight sleeping bags and knapsacks at specialty hiking stores. Ask for them. Below is a modified list of what I carried in the spring of 2008:

- Two pairs of hiking pants, preferably one pair that unzipped to become shorts
- one cotton T-shirt
- one quick dry wick away shirt, one jacket (preferably fleece)
- one pocket rain poncho
- three underwear, (choose bright colours, it took forever to find my black ones on the line!)
- three pairs of Merino wool hiking socks
- comfortable hiking boots
- flip-flops, (crocs are great too!)
- a sarong (helpful as a towel or housecoat)
- swim suit
- a quick dry hiking towel
- a head lamp
- sun block
- soap
- shampoo and sundries including
  » moleskin
  » scissors
  » Band-Aids

- » Traumeel
- » Arnica
- » Advil
- » Peppermint Foot Cream
- a water bottle
- a journal
- a book to read
- an iPod and camera, or one cell phone that does all of the above
- a plastic bag and mini bungee cord for laundry,
- a hat
- bandana
- walking stick

…and you're set. Buen Camino!

DAY ONE | *Es Su Camino*

At the start of every day in the meditation *ghompa* in Nepal, Lama Yeshe would remind us to set our intention. In Tibetan Buddhism, one always says a prayer of motivation before embarking on any endeavour. It's a bit like saying grace before dinner. It aids spiritual digestion. Also, the more committed we are to our intention the greater chances we have of achieving it. In the Mahayana tradition, we hope that any practices we might do will not only benefit ourselves, but also benefit everyone who comes into contact with us. After all, happiness like humour, is contagious.

Before we start the Camino, we usually have a lot of questions; where to start, how long to walk, and who to walk with, for instance. While walking The Way I often ran into pilgrims struggling with whether to travel with friends or walk alone. I did both. I walked with my husband for two weeks, walked alone, then fell in with other meditators who walked as slowly as myself. Along the route, I met a Dutch woman, who had walked the Camino many times. Her sage advice: "Better to walk by yourself and find your own Camino family. *Es Su Camino*. It's your walk. Do it the way you want."

A woman who worked for years with the dying wrote a list of the top five regrets people shared on their death beds. The number one regret was not living a life true to themselves. Here's your chance: It's your Camino. Make it wild, make it glorious, make it solo and introspective or raucous with new friends, but make it meaningful to you.

SIMPLE BREATHING MEDITATION

Start simply by noticing the air entering your nostrils. Relax. You don't have to do anything special, breathing is automatic. When your mind wanders gently bring it back to the breath at the nostrils, without self-recrimination or blame. Practice this for five minutes. Then five minutes more.

JOURNAL EXERCISE

At the end of the day sit down with your journal and ask yourself the following questions: Why are you walking? What is your intention? What do you hope this walk will do for you? What in your life is out of your control or in crisis? What are you powerless over? Are you struggling over the recent death of a loved one, a lost desire, a failed dream? Are you addicted to cigarettes, alcohol, weight loss, unrequited love? What do you want to focus on? How can you make this truly your Camino?

DAY TWO | *Siga Las Flechas or Follow the Arrows*

I flew halfway around the world, but on my first morning, I suddenly realized I had no idea how to begin my pilgrimage. Sheepishly, I asked the elegant young woman at the front desk of the hotel where to start the Camino.

"The Compostela?" the clerk asked. "*No problema*. You go out the hotel, turn right and the eros are there."

"The eros?"

"Yes, you follow the eros."

"Oh arrows."

"Excuse my English."

"Hey, it's better than my Spanish. I won't get lost?"

"I don't know if you will get lost," she said wisely. "But I think you will not. You follow the arrows all the way. It's easy... you will see," she said.

I smiled and thanked her in Spanish and heaved my pack onto my back and clattered down the cobblestone streets of Pamplona. It was as the desk clerk said. At the end of the street on a lovely stone wall I saw my first painted yellow arrow. I followed. Then I followed the one after that. Amazingly, the yellow arrows were almost always there, flashing brightly, pointing the way, like silent spiritual friends.

On every other stone wall, curbside and building on the Camino de Santiago, one finds painted yellow arrows, or blue conch shells pointing to Santiago. If we stop someone and ask for directions, they will often say: *Siga las fleches.*

Success in many ventures is often as simple as following direction. On the spiritual path, we study meditation from a master. In recovery, we get a sponsor. If we go hiking, we consult a map. We surrender our will and do what the teacher suggests. One step at a time. One arrow at a time.

This can be harder than it seems at first. Before learning surrender, we try to do everything ourselves. We tend to worry and doubt. On the Camino whenever someone was stuck or confused, the pilgrims would joke: *Follow the arrows*. It meant keep it simple, trust the process, take one problem at a time, one arrow at a time, one step at a time, one meditation at a time, and things will usually sort themselves out.

BODY SCAN MEDITATION

Walk while inhaling and gently exhaling. Keep your head still while your arms swing. Rest your tongue lightly on the roof of your mouth. Steady your eyes on the ground a few feet in front of you. Focus on the air entering your nostrils for a few minutes. Now shift your attention to your body as you walk, starting with your feet. How are they this morning? Feel your soles touching the ground. Now move up to your calves, knees, thighs, belly, heart—all the way up to your head. Breathe into each section, really feel whatever is there. Where are you holding tension? Breathe into any creaky bits. Give yourself permission to fully inhabit this body. It's your home for this life, this walk. Practice this for ten minutes, first thing in the morning.

DAY THREE | *Follow the Eros*

That first day as I walked through the rain, I couldn't stop chuckling about how I had mistaken arrows for eros when the desk clerk had spoken to me. Someone had once told me, there are no coincidences in life. Maybe one should also follow the *eros*? What would it mean to follow what we love in the broadest sense, to follow one's joy, to follow the heart's longing? To follow one's dream or bliss as Joseph Campbell once wrote. I'd been swamped with memories of the past, struggles with addiction, work and family responsibilities for years and had forgotten to pay attention to what was numinous, inspiring, and nourishing for my soul. I spent most of my life rushing around being busy, or distracting myself to alleviate pain, so, I rarely thought about what brought me joy.

One day I wandered into a beautiful town by a stream. There was a restaurant overlooking a waterfall. A small sign said: *Rooms for rent.* I was enchanted and lingered on the bridge. I wanted to stay but had already made plans to stop in the next town. The next town might be better, I told myself, and walked on. I ended out spending that night in a large, noisy city, regretting that I'd not jumped at the chance to rent a room by that burbling stream. I hadn't listened to my heart. I resolved from then on, to never rush past a beautiful place, to linger where there was beauty and magic. To follow my heart.

BREATHING MEDITATION
FOR BUILDING CONFIDENCE

Start the morning with five minutes of simple breathing practice, followed by five minutes of the Body Scan. Now we will move to a four-part breath: Inhale, then pause, exhale then briefly pause and start again. Focusing on all four parts of the breath equally builds confidence, balance, and stability. Relish each step of this rhythm. Don't hold the pause for too long. It should feel natural. Practice for ten minutes.

JOURNAL EXERCISE

Draw a circle on a piece of paper in your journal. Divide the circle into pie segments. This is the mandala of your life. Give each pie a heading: Career, family, friends, significant other, romance, fun and recreation, creativity, health, money, personal growth, spirituality and physical environment. Rate each one from 1-10 according to your level of satisfaction. One is low and 10 is high. Which areas are high, which are low? Where is your life out of balance? Which areas do you want to empower? What is your heart longing for? What *eros* do you want to follow? Pick one or two to focus on. They are your spiritual work for the next 30 days.

DAY FOUR | *Be Kind To Your Feet*

Accoring to reflexology, there are over seven thousand nerve endings in the feet. They connect by way of meridians to the spinal cord, brain and all the major organs of the body. That is why Traditional Chinese Medicine doctors sometimes suggest walking barefoot on cobblestones to recover from illness or injury; why walking for long distances can be so profoundly healing.

My first few days of walking, I noticed that every other pilgrim conversation revolved around feet. Should one favor boots with ankle support or boots without? Were soft boots with aeration better than sturdy solid leather clunkers? My friend, a former Buddhist monk, told me he went to the most reputable hiking store in London and bought the best boots in the store. He paid a fortune but was comfortable. Jason, who had flown to the Camino on a lark from Israel, wore brand new Merrill boots he pillaged from an *alburgue's* Lost and Found, but he had no end of trouble. I met two women who walked in pink crocs. A man who swore by hiking sandals.

Whatever you do, don't start a long walk with brand new boots, everyone warned. In the end, after four trips to *Adventure Attic* I took my six-year-old Rockports. They were broken in but still hardly worn. I bought fancy microwavable inserts that I nuked and then stood on so they molded to my feet. Afterwards, the soles felt like pillows. I put Vaseline on my feet every morning and rubbed them with peppermint cream every night. Someone gave me the advice to take it easy the first few days because that's when you usually get blisters. "The moment you feel a hot spot forming, stop and deal with it," he said.

One morning after a long climb, I felt a twinge on my baby toe. At the first outdoor café I could find, I whipped off my boots and socks and cut some moleskin. I was embarrassed to administer to my naked feet in public, but the other pilgrims didn't mind. One nodded sympathetically, another asked to borrow my scissors.

MEDITATION REVIEW

Practice your breathing meditations plus the Body Scan for five minutes each. Do this three part warm-up every morning.

ACTION STEP

Take care of your feet. Invest in some comfy socks, good boots, the best of Band-Aids. After walking, lie down on a bed and rest your legs up against the wall. Rub your feet with peppermint cream at night. Treat them well and they will take you all the way to Santiago or anywhere you want to go.

DAY FIVE | *Honour Your Own Rhythm*

I met an Italian cook named Vittore, who blew out his knee while walking the Pyrenees on his first day. He'd walked 35 kilometres straight up a massive hill with barely a rest, trying to keep up with a more experienced hiker. I learned from him that pushing the river only leads to injury. Every time I tried to keep up with others, I only ended out hurting myself, or hating them. Neither was a good idea. It is 778-kilometers to Santiago, which is not a sprint but an endurance test. Within the first few days I figured out that if I wanted to make it there, I was going to have to conserve energy and avoid injury. Behave like the tortoise, rather than the hare.

Also, I didn't fly all the way to Spain to rush and keep to a schedule. I could rush around at home. The reason why most people walk the Camino, is because they want to go on a spiritual journey. Part of that is getting to know ourselves, honouring our own bodies, deepening our connection to Higher Power and our own inner knowing. None of these things are achieved by rushing. When I rush, I'm usually focusing on the future, the goal, rather than being present to enjoy the process. As the Buddha said: *It is better to travel well than arrive.* Sometimes walking at our own pace is the kindest thing we can do for ourselves.

BREATHING MEDITATION
FOR ALLEVIATING ANXIETY

Once again focus on the breath entering your nostrils. Walk at your own pace. Notice when you start to rush. Does your breath quicken? Your chest tighten? While you walk, let your breathing be natural, relaxed. Don't force anything. *Force closes the heart.* Gradually shift your focus to your exhale. Gently elongate the exhale, just a little, then let go and inhale naturally. Does this automatically deepen your inhalation? Do you feel more relaxed? This will slow your pace and calm any anxiety. Practice this technique for ten minutes.

JOURNAL EXERCISE

Write about how you could honour your own rhythm in your life. When and why do you rush? How does your body feel when you rush? Typically, are you the tortoise or the hare?

DAY SIX | *Carry Only What You Need*

After Vittore the cook had blown out his knee walking the Pyrenees, he convalesced in an albergue for two days. There a Frenchman had taken one look at his pack and told him he had injured himself by carrying too much weight. The Frenchman went through Vittore's knapsack, tossing every second thing, shouting: "Inutile, inutile, inutile!"

"Useless, you don't need it! He even threw out my favourite shirt," Vittore exclaimed. "It was a denim shirt I'd had with me since the childhood years. I loved that shirt."

Vittore shook his head sadly. "Two shirts only, the Frenchman insisted."

I was just as foolish. I had stuffed my knapsack to the brim with extra T-shirts and sweaters, a heavy raincoat, cotton jacket, a hard cover journal. Ten kilos is often recommended, but I was carrying 12 and it felt like a small refrigerator after several hours. By the third day I knew I had to get rid of the extra weight. I left my blue jeans, the journal and some T-shirts in an alburgue in Estella.

A wonderful Feng Shui master named Tracy Stanton once told me that everything you keep that you don't love and no longer serves you is weighing you down. She had decluttering down to an art form. "Ask yourself three questions of everything you own," she said: "Do you love it? Is it useful? When you look at it, does it lift your spirit or energy in some way?"

MEDITATION FOR WAKING UP THE MIND

Practice simple nostril breathing and the Body Scan. Now shift your focus to your inhale. Breathe naturally but notice when the inhalation ends, that split second where inhalation turns into exhalation. Notice how paying attention to that one ascending event tends to make the mind more alert. Try this for ten minutes or when especially sleepy throughout the day.

ACTION STEP

Go through your knapsack at night or declutter a closet at home. Of every object ask yourself Tracy's three questions: Do you love it? Is it useful? Does it energize you? If it doesn't have two out of three of these qualities, let it go. What else are you carrying that no longer serves you? What emotional baggage? Ask yourself: Why am I still carrying this? What am I getting out of it? If it's a negative emotion, habit, worry or fault, pick up a stone. Visualize the habit penetrating the stone in your pocket. Carry the stone for the morning while walking, then when you're ready, leave it by the roadside. Let it go.

DAY SEVEN | *What Does Your Seigneur (or Source) Have to Say To You?*

At several of the towns along the Camino, the monks and nuns at the local monastaries would offer a pilgrim blessing. In Viana, the alburgue was actually part of the church. The church of Santa Maria was cathedral-sized with an enormous gold altar. Columns vaulted heavenward, as though defying gravity. There were panels with different tableaus that reminded me of Buddhist Tangka's, Tibetan religious paintings. I was amazed by how similar the images were in these very different spiritual traditions.

There was a Latin Mass. Toward the end, the Father, a handsome, serious man, invited all the pilgrims to come up to the dias. We pilgrims limped forward, unwashed and ragged after a day of slogging through mud and rain. Father had us form a circle. He spoke to us in English and Spanish.

"I have three advices from your Seigneur on your Camino," he said. "First one: Take a moment of silence every day, at least twenty minutes and listen to God. He has things he wants to say to you. Two: Take care of each other, you are on this trek together. Thirdly, take care of the environment around you, leave it neat and clean for the pilgrims who come after you."

For years I was uncomfortable with the word God. Finally, I fired the punishing God from my childhood and replaced it with a Higher Power or Source that worked for me. It is said that prayer is petitioning God, while meditation is listening for the answer. In Buddhism, we were taught to sit in silence with an open heart and wait for those aha! moments, those little epiphanies that arise from the stillness, like messages from the Divine. This was much easier once I had a concept I could relate to.

LISTENING TO SOURCE MEDITATION

As you walk in silence visualize your Spiritual Source above your head. Let the Infinite appear in any way that feels natural to you. If you don't believe in a Higher Power, visualize radiant light. As you walk, breathe in this white light, feel this compassionate energy entering the top of your head at your crown chakra. While you walk, breathe in this Divine Light. Does it have a colour, a shape, a sound? Practice this for 15 minutes. After a time, notice if your Source has anything to say to you. Do any epiphanies or messages arise?

JOURNAL EXERCISE

Write a one-page biography of your spiritual beliefs, including your relationship with God, Source, or Higher Power. How is that relationship working for you? If you had to fire your old God, what would your new Source be like? If you don't believe in enlightened beings, what do you believe? Who are your greatest heroes? Who inspires you? Who would you like to emulate: Mother Theresa? Mahatma Gandhi? Malcolm X?

DAY EIGHT | *The Bigger the Mountain, the Smaller the Steps*

On my first week walking the Camino I walked with my husband and some expats from Paris. Soon we came upon *Bodega Irache*, a famous Benedictine monastery with a wine museum that offered free wine to pilgrims. The others helped themselves, but I was abstaining from drinking for the duration of the walk, wrestling with whether or not I was an alcoholic. They had fun filling up their water bottles. Afterwards we climbed a relentlessly steep hill. I grew depressed. I had asthma as a child so have always hated steep inclines. Plus I worried that my life would never be fun again without alcohol. I had already given up desserts and white sugar. How would I manage to get through life? They sprinted on ahead while I lumbered slowly upwards. My pack was too heavy, the hill was steep, my Achilles tendons were aching. Every time I looked up at the top, I despaired about how far I had to go. Finally, when I was on the verge of tears, I stopped, and turned around, so that they wouldn't see me crying.

Suddenly I was greeted with a magnificent view. It was miraculous. I saw how far I'd come. It dawned on me I should congratulate myself on what I'd accomplished rather than worry about what was still ahead. I resolved while climbing, to watch my feet, to concentrate only on the next few steps in front of me. I stopped struggling with the incline and began zigzagging taking baby steps. Whenever my calves began to burn, I stopped, turned around to enjoy the view and patted myself on the back. In this way, I managed to inch myself up that massive incline without misery and was surprised and thrilled when I reached the top. Now every time I feel daunted by a challenge, I try to remind myself: The bigger the hill, the smaller the steps.

MEDITATION REVIEW

Do five minutes of the Body Scan and a breathing meditation of your choice. Followed by 15 minutes of the previous Listening to Source meditation. Continue this practice for the next few days.

JOURNAL EXERCISE

Here are today's questions: What is the biggest problem you have right now? What are you obsessing about? How could you break this problem down into smaller more manageable steps?

DAY NINE | *Gratitude is the Greatest of Virtues*

One morning in the hilly mountain town of Villafranca, I asked an elderly pilgrim how he was doing. His response was: "Every day above ground is a gift."

When I was at the monastery in Kopan, Nepal, in the 1970s, we were taught the Lam Rim, a series of foundation teachings in Buddhism. There was an important early teaching called the Perfect Human Rebirth. Buddhists believe that they have reincarnated countless times, but do not always have the opportunity of a human rebirth. Whether you believe in reincarnation or not the underlying principle is universal—that essentially human life is a gift. Lama Yeshe stressed that as human beings we can learn, study spiritual teachings, and improve our minds. We can practice altruism and compassion and achieve enlightenment or awakening.

The Roman philosopher Marcus Tullius Cicero said: *Gratitude is not only the greatest of virtues, it is the parent of all others.* So, in many spiritual disciplines, gratitude for one's life is a prerequisite to happiness. Often addicts in recovery are asked to keep a gratitude journal. There are several reasons for this. When we focus on the glass half empty, we notice only what is not working in our lives and despair. If we focus on the glass half full, on what is working, we feel more positive and more open to discovering creative solutions. This is especially important, because according to the *Law of Attraction*, whatever we focus on grows. The Hindu Prince Gautama Siddhartha, 563-483

B.C., who became known as the Buddha encapsulated this idea in the following quote: *All that we are is the result of what we have thought. The mind is everything. What we think we become.*

GRATITUDE MEDITATION

Repeat the previous day's meditation instructions, practicing for twenty minutes. Only this time as you breathe in Source's white healing light, breathe in gratitude, exhale complaint, dissatisfaction, disease.

JOURNAL EXERCISE

Write a list of 10 things you are grateful for today.

DAY TEN | *Thinking Is Free,*
Breathing is Free, God is Free

My husband walked with me for the first two weeks of my journey. After our tearful goodbye at the train station in Burgos, I planned to continue alone. I was gloomy the next morning, afraid to walk by myself. I had slept in and set out late, as the stores were slowly opening up, and vendors hosed down the cobblestones. I began climbing out of the ancient city, the cathedral with its leather Jesus receding behind me, doubting the whole enterprise, afraid I wouldn't find friends to accompany me.

Everyone had already left, pilgrims typically rose early, so I saw no one for a while. I had only the yellow arrows for company. At a café on the outskirts of town, I passed a garbage container, *un vidrio,* splattered with graffiti that read:

Pensar es libre
Respirar es libre
Dios es libre

Thinking is free.
Breathing is free.
God is free.

This message startled me out of my gloom. I suddenly knew what to do. I had to connect with Source, breathe in white light, exhale my fearful thoughts, my sad thoughts. Turn these fears over to Higher Power and pray for help. As soon as I focused on my practice my spirits lifted, my optimism returned.

I followed an old rail trail through an open field bordered by highways. Crickets scratched their legs in the long grass, while trucks lumbered above. In the shade of an underpass, I stopped to have a snack of apple and cheese. I had to pee. I managed to do up my pants just in time to hear a fellow pilgrim calling me: "Hey K, come join us! I've met some Canadians!"

SOURCE MANTRA MEDITATION

Begin with a breathing practice for 15 minutes. Now, visualize your Higher Power. Allow It/Her/Him to appear in any way that is comfortable. Visualize Source sending love to warm your heart. Put your hand on your heart to strengthen this connection or touch your first finger to the tip of your thumb in the mudra for connecting with the Divine. Repeat: *God is with me, God is guiding me, God is helping me.* Or change the words to suit: Source is with me, Buddha is helping me, Higher Consciousness is guiding me, etc. Continue this practice for 15 minutes.

DAY ELEVEN | *The Camino Provides*

I lost my socks one day on the Camino. I'd spent the night in Fromista, in a crowded alburgue in a vacated school. When I went to get my laundry off the line in the morning, I discovered that someone, whether by accident or not, had taken my socks. My favourite Merino wool socks. They were olive green and I loved them. I panicked and began rushing up and down the line, scouring the laundry for my favourite socks but they were nowhere to be found.

The Buddha warned about the dangers of attachment. He taught that we continually seek happiness in things outside ourselves and become miserable when separated from them. When I lost my socks, for a few minutes I wanted to cry. My mind went wild, catastrophizing, imagining tragic scenarios: I only had two pair left, what would I do if I got caught in the rain and my second pair didn't dry overnight? Then I remembered an expression another pilgrim had shared with me: *The Camino provides*.

I decided to pray and meditate on this. I will be okay, I told myself. *This too shall pass.* They're only socks, after all. Note to Source I prayed, *Please send me a new pair of socks.*

That afternoon I stopped for a lemonade at a little roadside café. Soon two friends recognized me and stopped also. I told them of my missing socks.

Havier said, "Oh K, don't worry I have five pairs I will give you one of mine."

I accepted a lovely pair of steel blue socks with white silk inserts from Havier. They were fancier than the ones I'd had before, the Cadillac of socks. I wore Havier's socks for the rest of the journey. Every time I put them on I thought of his kindness, and how the Camino provides when we remember to ask for help.

MEDITATION REVIEW

Continue with Source Mantra Meditation for a half an hour each morning for the next days.

ACTION STEP

Pray for divine guidance about a problem. Once you've prayed about it, let it go. Ask for help from others and allow the Camino to provide.

DAY TWELVE | *Une Revision de Vie or Review Your Life*

E arly on in my trip, I was halfway to the top of *Alto del Perdon*, when I met an Alsatian *peregrina,* a female pilgrim, who was sitting on a picnic bench, peeling an apple. I was exhausted and asked if my husband and I might join her.

"*Avec plaisir,*" she said. We chitchatted, sharing cashews and apples and the usual Camino conversation. What's your name? Where are you from? Where did you start walking? Why are you really walking? Her husband had recently died. I shared that I had turned fifty and wanted to do something special to celebrate having lived that long and take some time to think about the next steps in my life.

"So you have embarked on a *revision de vie,*" the French woman said.

A life review. What a concept!

That afternoon after we'd said goodbye, I struggled up the long hill to Alto del Perdon. It was windy and raining, I was bent over like a Sherpa to keep from slipping on the wet ground. While walking, inevitably, I began thinking about my past, my life, about the choices I had made or didn't make. For the rest of the journey, my husband and I did a life review to pass the time. We began by sharing our childhood in five-year increments: What life was like, where we lived, as well as major events, memories and significant relationships with siblings, parents, extended family, and friends. We shared whether we were happy, sad, or felt loved; and shared funny stories of our early years. The more we shared, the closer we became and the more unburdened I felt.

When we got to the small plateau that was Alto del Perdon, with its bronze monument to the pilgrim's journey, the sun broke through, shining on the silhouettes of ancient pilgrims. It reminded us of the river of humanity that had walked this same route for over a thousand years.

JOURNAL EXERCISE

Begin your life review. Jot down the major events of your life story in point form on a page. Just the bare bones. What were the major turning points? The major wounds? Mark a cross when someone died or a star when a dream was born. Include your accomplishments, forks in the road. When you read it over, are there any situations left unresolved? Words unsaid? Things you wished you had done?

DAY THIRTEEN | *Wash Your Socks*

E very day after walking the Camino, the first thing pilgrims did was their laundry. One afternoon I arrived late at the alburgue in the pouring rain. There was one room devoted to laundry tubs and clotheslines, but it was packed to the brim with wet hiking gear. I could barely find space on the line. The next morning my clothes were still wet. I had to carry wet socks and soggy pants attached to the outside of my pack with bungee cords. They were incredibly heavy. I had learned a lesson: Arrive early enough to do laundry. Washing one's socks was a priority.

For a time I walked with Adam, who was a former Buddhist monk. One afternoon, we were discussing how when people first discover meditation they often go through a period of initial ease and bliss. Adam told me it's called a pink cloud. I shared that in recovery there was something called pink cloud abstinence. Adam went on to tell me about the Buddhist writer Jack Kornfield. One of his books is titled, *After the Ecstasy, the Laundry.* In it Kornfield explains how when the pink cloud wears off at some point what we're faced with is laundry, the hum drum, nitty gritty chores of life.

"On the Camino, all we do is laundry," I said.

"I know," Adam agreed, "I've never done more laundry in my life!"

I decided there was a reason we had to do so much laundry on the Camino. It was part of the purification, the psychic house cleaning. As our feet hit the ground, we were detoxing and purifying our bodies, massaging the seven thousand reflexology points in our feet. But when we prayed and meditated while walking, the cleansing was also emotional and spiritual. In our regular rush-rush world, we wash our clothes, our hair, our cars, but we rarely clean up what's inside. We forget to practice what my Buddhist therapist Susan W. used to call: *Mental hygiene.*

JOURNAL EXERCISE

How is your mental and emotional hygiene? Do your thoughts revolve around fear?

In your journal write down three major fears. What do you imagine is the worst that could happen? What could you do to prevent the worst from happening, if anything? And what is the best thing that could happen to resolve this fear? Pick an image that epitomizes that solution for you and focus on it whenever you begin to worry about this fear again.

DAY FOURTEEN | *Spiritual Friends*

angha in Buddhism is the Sanskrit word for assembly or spiritual community. In the Tibetan Buddhist tradition, we begin meditation by taking refuge. To take refuge means to take comfort in the dharma or spiritual teachings. The prayer goes like this: *I take refuge in the Buddha, the Dharma, the Sangha.* Sometimes I like to translate this prayer into more general terms: *I take refuge in the inspiration, the teachings, and my spiritual friends.*

Similarly, in recovery it is recommended that you make program friends to help you along the spiritual path. You find a sponsor who acts as a mentor to you. Someone who will guide you along the way so that you don't get stuck in your loneliness or despair; someone who will show you compassion, while you are learning to have compassion for yourself. A sponsor often becomes a good friend.

In *Anam Cara: A Book of Celtic Wisdom* by John O'Donohue, he writes: *In everyone's life, there is a great need for an anam cara, a soul friend.* This soul friend in the Celtic tradition was originally someone we confessed or told our secrets too; someone with whom we could share the inner most stirrings of our heart; who listened with kindness and accepted us as we are.

In the long hours of walking the Camino, there is an opportunity to share with other pilgrims like no other place on earth; an opportunity to make special friends, soul friends, spiritual friends.

LOVING KINDNESS FOR SELF MEDITATION

Higher Power is your ultimate spiritual friend. Imagine Source appearing above your head sending you love and compassion and acceptance in the form of white light. This light enters your body, filling your head, throat, belly, torso, pelvis, arms, and legs. Inhale this loving white light and exhale your fear or discontent in the form of black smoke. Practice this for half an hour.

ACTION STEP

If you could have a spiritual friend who would that be? What qualities would that friend have? Notice if there's anyone on the road or in your life with whom you feel that reciprocity. Reach out to someone who makes you feel understood.

DAY FIFTEEN | *Sharing*

I n the infamous Buddhist *Parable of the Mustard Seed*, a mother loses her only child. Grief stricken, she rushes into the local town and begs for help. She goes from merchant to merchant, her hair wild, streaked with rain, the child decomposing in her arms, asking if anyone knows the cure for death. Finally, someone recommends that she speak to Gautama Buddha.

She goes to Jeta Grove where the Buddha is teaching and lays the rotting corpse of her infant in front of him, begging Gautama to tell her the cure for death.

"My husband is wealthy," she says, "I will pay you anything!"

The Buddha tells her that he does know a cure for death. It will require one mustard seed from the house that has experienced no death. He tells her: "If you bring me this, I will prepare the cure."

The woman goes from house to house roaming near and far, through relentless rain and withering heat, looking for that elusive abode that has experienced no death. But at each door she knocks she hears the same lament: *My father died only four months ago. My sister and brothers have all passed. My son was killed at war.* Murdered. Drowned. On and on goes the litany of human suffering. Finally, the mother gives up searching, accepts her loss and comes to understand the Buddha's teaching on impermanence and the inevitability of death.

One by one the people we love will die until we die ourselves. Death is inevitable. I like to think though, that the grieving mother is healed in the end, by telling her story again and again, and listening to the stories of others. By sharing our sorrow, we are healed of our isolation. Perhaps, that is the only mustard seed, the only cure for death there is.

MEDITATION REVIEW

Begin each morning with 15 minutes of breathing meditations, followed by 15 minutes of Loving Kindness Meditation. Continue this practice for two days.

JOURNAL EXERCISE

Write down three things that make you angry in your life.

ACTION STEP

Find a spiritual friend with kind ears, someone on a compatible spiritual path. Share some portion of your life story. Ask if you can share with them some of your fears or things that make you angry. Ask them to listen without comment or judgment. Thank them for listening.

DAY SIXTEEN | *In God's Time*

While walking, I met a group of women expats who were living in Paris. They belonged to a walking club that took train trips to the outskirts of the city every Sunday so that members could go exploring by foot. They were walking the Camino together for a week.

"You get to know a place in a special way when you walk through it," one of the women said to me. She had been born in South Africa and had lived in several other African countries. I nicknamed her Zimbabwe.

Perhaps, it's because walking is in God's time, I thought. While walking you take the time to breathe, to think, to look around. Many pilgrims claim they feel a special bond with northern Spain because they discovered it by walking. The Camino is forever associated with beauty, restfulness, and expansiveness. For centuries our ancestors walked everywhere. The car is a relatively modern invention. Walking connects our feet to Mother Earth. We draw energy from connecting to the ground. Are healed in fact by each step we take across her terrain. The mind can rest while walking and so connects us to a different sense of time: God's time.

I've often felt frustrated by how long it takes to resolve certain difficulties in life. Why was it so hard to kick a certain habit? Why did my depression and gloominess linger? It took me seven years just to quit smoking! My dreams never came true on schedule! Walking teaches us patience, to surrender to God's time. As the expression goes: *All good things happen in God's time.*

JOURNAL EXERCISE

What do you wish you could change about your life? What fault, habit, or life problem would you like to change? Think of something that you successfully changed in the past. How long did it take?

ACTION STEP

Don't look at your watch for an entire day. Notice how things get done all the same.

DAY SEVENTEEN | *The Heart Has No Wrinkles, Only Scars—Collette*

e coeur n'as pas de rides, il n'y a que les cicatrices," my French-speaking friend from Zimbabwe told me. It was a quote from the famous French author Collette. *The heart has no wrinkles, only scars.*

While walking below a field of wind turbines one day, we talked about aging. How even though we were now middle-aged women, we often felt like teenagers: We still got crushes, fell in love. She confessed she'd been married three times. "Even though we get old, our heart does not get old," she told me. "In our minds we remain forever young."

How wonderful I thought. The heart is ageless. We get scars but we still feel like we're thirty even when we're fifty. Maybe, the heart has no wrinkles because it's renewable. A renewable resource. The heart can grow and heal and change. Even when we are heartbroken eventually the sorrow passes. In time we recover, and we are never too old to love.

In Tibetan Buddhism, the heart is often referred to as the mind. The mind is not located in the head as it is in western culture. The Tibetans suggest we should make decisions using our higher mind, meaning "our heart," because the heart makes better decisions. The English language is full of heartfelt expressions that support this view: The heart of the matter, follow your heart, a path with heart. Perhaps on the Camino, the heart should guide the feet. The heart should decide, left, right, stop, go. Who to talk to, who to walk with.

LOVING KINDNESS MEDITATION
FOR TRANSFORMING FEAR

Take out your sheet of fears. Read them. Which one most troubles your heart? As you walk visualize Higher Power above your head. Pick one fear that you would like to be free of. Ask your Source: *May I be free of* ... now fill in the blank. Then conclude with: *May I be at peace.* You might repeat: *May I be free of fear.* Pray to be free of whatever hurts your heart: fear of poverty, terror of your childhood abuser, fear of being left by your significant other, of never getting justice or rewarded for your work, whatever interferes with your serenity. Get very specific. Repeat your mantra silently while walking. Inhale: *May I be free of....* Exhale: *May I be at peace.* Allow whatever feelings arise. You are purifying. Cry all morning if you need too. You are healing your renewable heart.

DAY EIGHTEEN | *Your Happy Talisman*

I was struggling up a long hill one morning, stiff, and sore, full of bitter and resentful thoughts, my mind a cesspool of self-pity. Then I remembered a crinkled piece of paper I kept on my altar at home. It was a sheet from the Louise L. Hay Educational Institute that someone had given me at a workshop. It was called, *How to Love Yourself.* As hokey as that sounds, I've found loving myself a lifelong challenge. It included a series of ten steps for a happy mind. The one that struck me was number two, where Ms. Hay tells us to stop scaring ourselves with frightening thoughts. She recommends replacing a frightening thought with a mental image that gives us pleasure.

I wondered, what that happy talisman could be for me. I couldn't think of anything in that moment that made me happy. So, I looked around. Beside me was an enormous stone wall. I examined it for a moment before I realized that it was covered by wild climbing roses, crimson-coloured, and voluptuous. I took a few steps closer. There were more roses spilling out of a wrought iron fence. They were intoxicating and everywhere, a happy consequence of all the rain. I was touched by their fragility. Instinctively, I stuck my nose in one of the fleshy centers. The smell was sweet and hopeful. My cheek was gently caressed by the skin-like petals. They startled me out of my unhappiness. Who could be unhappy in the face of such simple beauty? I resolved to smell a rose every day. I would stop and sniff whenever I felt sad and was surprised each time by how their beauty gave me such solace.

Pick a happy talisman or a happy place. Something or some place that makes your mind happy just to think about: A beach, Spain's red climbing roses, hot chocolate, the dock at the cottage, whatever. Whenever you feel disturbed or sad during the day conjure this uplifting image or place and hold it in your mind until your discouragement evaporates.

DAY NINETEEN | *When It Rains the Pack is Less Heavy!*

My husband and I were staying in an old monastery in Santo Domingo with a bunkroom that housed chickens in a cage for the church next door. That day it poured and poured. We were assigned bunk beds lined up cheek to jowl. There was a wine festival going on: Fiesta Rioja. People got in late, drunk, and their snoring filled the rafters. We had hastily washed our clothes and left them out on the line before bed. In the morning we awakened to pouring rain and all our clean hiking gear was soaked. We were devastated. We would have to walk through the rain carrying heavy laundry for an entire day. We had slept in and were among the last to leave. In one corner there was a morose Frenchman slowly packing up his stuff. He was putting on all the clothes in his pack to stay warm.

"*Meme quand il pleut, le sac est plus legere,*" he said, as if to comfort himself. At least when it rains the pack is less heavy.

I laughed out loud. Later I thought of the cliché that every cloud has a silver lining and wondered what this one would be. Life is a paradox. The good times come with dangerous excesses, and the bad times come with important lessons. Sue, my recovery friend once told me: "There's a gift in every challenge, even if you have to look really hard to find it."

Over breakfast at a little café that rainy morning, we watched the weather on TV. Spain was having the worst rain in fifty years. We would be drenched if we walked anywhere and unable to get our clothes dry. We decided then and there to have a duvet day. From then on, we scheduled weekly duvet days. Rest days. Everyone needs a reprieve, a day under the covers doing nothing. I made it part of my spiritual practice.

LOVING KINDNESS MEDITATION FOR SELF AND OTHERS

As you walk visualize Source sending you unconditional love. Are you angry? Overtired? Distrustful? Do you feel unworthy of love? Notice any criticisms or negative self-talk that gets in the way of receiving loving kindness for yourself. Breathe them out as dark smoke and watch them dissipate into thin air. If you find this difficult, imagine yourself as a helpless infant. Breathe in loving kindness for that child, then breathe out whatever gets in the way.

Now share your loving kindness with someone else. Think of one good friend, someone you care about, but are not romantically involved with. It could be your spiritual friend or *anam cara*. Pray for them: *May Cindy be free of suffering. May Cindy be at peace.* Walk with this for a while. Visualize your friend surrounded by light and love sent from your warm heart.

ACTION STEP

What is the kindest thing you can do for yourself today? Is it time for a duvet day? For rest? For a massage? For fun? When you are kinder to yourself, how do you feel about others?

DAY TWENTY | *How You Walk the Camino, is How You Are in Life*

I set out one morning in the rain, miserable because I hadn't had my *café con leche*. I had hoped to run into my friends Adam and Jason, but there was no one about. I climbed and climbed through rain and wind, up a long endless hill, my poncho flailing about me, my boots sticking in the boggy red clay. All the way I watched my grouchy thoughts. I tried to let go of my negative thoughts, my faults: Attachment to coffee, to getting my own way. But the more I thought about my failings the more there were. I started this walk with the trusty few, the loyal ones: Pride, self-pity, depression, gloominess, resentments galore. I did my best to dissolve them with white light but all my spiritual tools failed me on this morning. I was sad, full of fears about the future. Maybe it was the Milky Way. The field of stars above me, magnifying all my flaws so that I would finally see them and weep my way to Santiago where I would eventually leave them once and for all. But I was no longer that naïve. Wherever I went my faults followed.

At the top of the hill, some French pilgrims huddled complaining about the miserable weather. My hardy Australian friend Arilda was there waiting for me.

"Quit your whinging," she told them. "If it was 35 degrees Celsius you'd be sweating your butts off and complaining about that I reckon. You should be grateful it's cool."

I laughed. I remembered another Camino wisdom I'd heard on the trail: *How you walk the Camino, is how you are in life.*

How true, I thought. The only cure for complaining was acceptance: Acceptance of a morning without coffee, acceptance of the rain, acceptance of self, grouchy or not.

WITNESSING MEDITATION

Begin with breathing practice for ten minutes. Now turn your attention to your thoughts. When they interrupt your serenity say: Thinking. If you find yourself listening, say listening, naming whatever arises: Smelling, plotting, fantasizing, fear, anger, sadness. Give every interruption a friendly name. No need to judge yourself. Let your thoughts come and go, just notice if they're fearful thoughts or happy thoughts. They have information for you. Remember you are bigger than your thoughts. Continue this practice for 15 minutes, every morning for the next few days.

JOURNAL EXERCISE

Write down a list of your worst faults and weaknesses in a column on the left-hand side of your journal. Think of every criticism everyone ever told you about you. List them. Then on the right side of the page, opposite each fault, write down its positive manifestation. For instance, stubbornness can also be tenacity. Perfectionism can be thoroughness. There is a profane and a sacred aspect to every quality. Finish your list. Remember: You are the way you are for a reason.

DAY TWENTY-ONE | *In the End It's All About Your Stuff*

I'd caught up with my friends Klaus and Adam and was having lunch at Mesa Le Cowboy. Plastic pink flamingos waded in the pond. Seventies rock and roll streamed out the windows. We sat at a white plastic table that sported a wide umbrella. Adam began unpacking his knapsack. As we sat transfixed, he carefully produced a small refrigerator's worth of food: Rice cakes, salami, pecorino cheese made from sheep's milk, a bag of cherries, dates and plums, finally a squashed peach. He laid his treasures out on the table. Klaus produced a bag of Himalayan salt and started pouring it into his palm. When I teased them, they asked me what I carried. I confessed to carrying things for my teeth. I had special brushes for my gums, soft picks, cardboard toothpicks, waxy mint-flavoured dental floss.

We laughed and teased each other about our idiosyncrasies, the funny things we carried; health food, snacks, dental accoutrements.

"It's all about the stuff in the end," Adam said. "It's all about our stuff."

"All the stuff," Klaus said. "What we're willing to carry and what we leave behind."

"Yes," I said, "the physical stuff and the emotional stuff, it all comes with and says so much about us."

TRANSFORMING QUALITIES MEDITATION

As you walk visualize your Higher Power once more as radiant white universal energy above your head. As you inhale, breathe in the positive qualities on the right-hand side of your list of qualities. Exhale the negative qualities as dark smoke. Inhale tenacity, exhale stubbornness. When finished, inhale acceptance, exhale peace.

ACTION STEP

Take another look at the stuff in your pack. What does it say about you? What are you still holding onto that no longer serves you?

DAY TWENTY-TWO |
The Ghosts of Pilgrims Past

One day, my new walking friend Sam and I stopped at a former pilgrim hospital that had been renovated and turned into a *refugio*. The alburgue was by a river and there was a lovely stream. After walking 17 kilometres or more we were tired and sore. I went down to the water to put my feet in the river. The water was deliciously cool: I let my feet soak. From where I sat, I could see an endless river of pilgrims crossing the bridge, stumbling into the little encampment. After a while a young Spanish pilgrim came to cool his feet in the river beside me. He spoke excellent English, so we began talking. He told me that the province of Galicia was known as Magical Galicia.

"Before Christianity came there were many *bruja's* here," he said. "How do you call that in English?"

"Witches," I offered.

"Yes, witches," he said. "Many *magi* also. Here in Galicia we are very superstitious. Have you heard of the *santa companas*?" he asked. "Watching the pilgrims cross the bridge reminds me of them. They are like spirits of the dead," he explained. "It is said if you see a pilgrim coming down the road at night with a candle, something bad will befall you. If you pass him on a bridge you must carry his cross for thirty days. We are very superstitious here. The *santa companas* are the spirits of the dead pilgrims and they are everywhere along the trip."

In life we are sometimes pursued by metaphorical ghosts: The ghosts of our regrets, our fears, our unfulfilled dreams, our unresolved relationships. They follow us like shadows wherever we go, until we face them and let them go.

LOVING KINDNESS FOR
DIFFICULT OTHERS MEDITATION

Visualize Source above your head once more, radiating loving kindness and acceptance. Ask yourself: Who are your *santa companas*, your ghosts of the past? Who annoys you? Whom do you fear or resent? Visualize the mother who abandoned you, the violent alcoholic father. Now visualize Source sending them the light of forgiveness. You are not condoning their actions by forgiving them. You are letting go of the hurt done to you. You don't have to do anything but be willing. Say silently: *May so and so be free of suffering. May he/she be at peace.*

ACTION STEP

Make an apology. Say you're sorry without excuses, rationalizations, or evasions to someone on your list of unresolved situations. If you can't see them in person or reach them by phone, write them a letter. Then burn it and let it go.

DAY TWENTY-THREE
A Good Place to Die

Halfway through the journey I hiked to a templar site called San Bol with an Australian woman named after a virgin martyr. I call her Arilda. She wore a red bandana, had two walking sticks and was sporty and lean. She had grown up in Europe and lived in Australia, sounded like a French Ozzie, and had a no-nonsense quality that I liked. We trekked up a long winding road, a big sky above, chatting all the way. She told me right off that she was a lesbian.

"I don't believe in beating around the bush," she said, "there isn't enough time for that."

Then she told me that her lover had run off with her best friend.

"I'm so sorry," I said, stricken at this news. I stopped to take a drink.

"I was asleep for eight years," she said, "I don't blame her."

"That's magnanimous of you."

"Shit happens," she said.

"Man, but that's tough."

"Well, there's nothing I can do about it is there, so I just have to get on with my life. No point sitting around feeling sorry for myself."

Right.

We spent that night sleeping under the stars at the abandoned templar hut. The next day it poured rain and we walked together some more. She confessed to me that she had an illness that might conceivably kill her. All along the route I had noticed crosses and wondered about them. Someone had finally explained that a small percentage of people actually died on the Camino. The next day we were walking into Castrojeritz, a beautiful old Roman town with Jason the musician. It had been an important pilgrim town with over seven hospitals at the beginning of the 19th century. We could see the sand-coloured church, looming out of the rocky landscape. In my guide book, it said there were two refugios to choose from so we decided to stop for the night.

"Doesn't it make you nervous the mention of all those hospitals?" Jason said. "It seems like people came on the Camino to die."

I winced knowing Arilda's situation. But I needn't have felt protective.

"It's as good a place to die as any, I reckon," Arilda said.

DEATH MEDITATION

As you walk notice your breath. Ask yourself: What if this were your last walk? What if your life ended when the Camino was over? What if you had only one year to live? What would be important to you? What would need to be finished? What would no longer matter at all? What could you take with you? What would you leave behind? If death came tomorrow, what would you do today?

DAY TWENTY-FOUR | *Detach with Love*

One day Zimbabwe and I were talking about our mothers; rather, our troubled relationships with our mothers. We both had difficult mothers we didn't feel close too. I told Zimbabwe how my mother had been unsympathetic about my sexual abuse as a child. My mother had not believed me or helped me when I sought justice. This stubborn unsympathetic stance had hurt me so deeply I'd found it difficult to forgive her.

"Detach with love," Zimbabwe advised. That's what a Buddhist teacher had told her. "Sometimes we need to let go of the people who cause us pain. But it's important to do it with love."

Because they are as imperfect as we are.

Later on in my ambulatory rehab I ended out walking for a long time with someone who was often ill. She wouldn't go to hospital or seek help, and she still drank and smoked occasionally. I was tempted to leave her on many occasions and felt confused about whether I was being co-dependent or helpful. Several people told me to leave her behind and carry on—it was my walk too after all. I did continue without her once or twice, but always went back for her. Many years later a program person told me that I should never do for someone else what they could do for themselves. "We must look out for one another, but not carry one another," she said. For when we fall into co-dependent relationships, we end out disempowering the other person, and shouldering a responsibility that was never ours to carry. As difficult as it is, sometimes we have to detach from toxic people in order to heal ourselves.

Journal about one difficult relationship in your life. Past or present. What happened? What was your part in the situation? How did you contribute to the difficulty even by omission? Did you act out in anger, pride, defensiveness, or evade and abandon the other person? Are any of these your old coping strategies? Like keeping silent in a violent alcoholic home. Can this relationship be repaired? Or is this someone you need to detach from with love?

THE WISHING TREE PURIFICATION

Write down the name of your difficult person on a piece of paper. Then fold the paper, punch a tiny hole in one corner. Now stick your prayer on a small branch on a tree. Give this person to the tree. Thank the tree. This person is no longer your concern.

DAY TWENTY-FIVE
You Are Not Your Thoughts

I walked through Galicia with my friend Sam, who was an art therapist. One day she told me she was struggling with negative thoughts. She related something a Buddhist friend had told her. She said there were three kinds of Buddhists: The angry ones, the greedy ones and the disillusioned.

I laughed: "Oh dear, I've been all three!"

Sam confessed to being one of the angry ones.

I remembered something my friend Pat Guillet, psychotherapist had told me. She said most people struggle with either self-righteous anger or self-pity while meditating. They are either furious for what someone else has done to them or full of grief and feel sorry for themselves.

At first this disturbed me—either option wasn't great. After a while, it gave me peace. When we walk in silence, we come face to face with our thoughts and sometimes that is painful. At least now I knew that it was normal to experience negativity. I could change it. Transform my thoughts. One of my Buddhist teachers, former nun Dekyi-Lee Oldershaw says we have 35-thousand thoughts a day; still we are not our thoughts. We are much more than our thoughts.

BLUE SKY MEDITATION

This was Adam the monk's favourite meditation. Visualize your mind as a blue sky. As you walk, thoughts come and go like fluffy clouds. They are whimsical, impermanent as the weather on the Camino, as impermanent as your moods, your thoughts. As you walk, try watching your thoughts. Let them come and go like those fluffy clouds, say hello, but don't let them carry you off. Return every time to your open spacious blue-sky mind, the breath gently coming and going.

DAY TWENTY-SIX | *God (Source) Has Already Forgiven You*

I went to a talk by a well-known Catholic priest who had once been a terrible alcoholic. He had gotten sober in recovery and was renowned for his talks. I entered a lovely, crowded church one summer night to hear him talk about forgiveness.

Father stood before the crowd and said: "If you are worried about forgiveness, I have good news for you. God has already forgiven you. It's your job to receive it. More important, it's an insult not to receive it."

He went on to encourage the assembly to think of the person who loved them most in this world and multiply that love ten times.

"That's the amount of love God has for you," he said.

I started to cry. The idea of being forgiven was so powerful. The moment I felt worthy of forgiveness, suddenly I felt so much more charitable toward others.

In the meditation tent long ago in Kopan, Nepal, Lama Yeshe told us one night that really we were enlightened already. We were born with Buddha nature. The mind in its essence was always pure, but in life obscurations came until we could no longer see the clear light. But it was always there. The true nature of the mind never changed. He talked about how we often beat ourselves up for our imperfections. And encouraged us to be kind to ourselves. For when we are, it's so much easier to be kind to somebody else.

FORGIVENESS MEDITATION

Imagine Higher Power once more above your head. This time as you walk, visualize Source sending you forgiveness. Feel this light of forgiveness cascading into the crown of your head, sending a warm shower of forgiveness down through your body, healing your thoughts, your speech, and finally your wounded heart. Everything you've said in anger, every omission of kindness, every ignorant mistake you've ever made is transformed by this warm forgiving light. Your suffering leaves your body in the form of dark smoke. If you find it difficult to accept this forgiveness, repeat the loving kindness mantra: *May I be free of guilt and shame. May I be forgiven.*

DAY TWENTY-SEVEN | *Keep Walking*

My husband walked 800 kilometres too. He walked the Bruce Trail in Ontario over many weekends and many years. When comparing the Camino de Santiago with the Bruce Trail he said, "It's not that the Camino is harder, it's just longer because most people do it all at once, so it takes more endurance to keep getting up every day and continue walking."

Jason the musician I met along the way would often ask: "Why are we walking? Why did we choose this?" He was joking but there were days I wondered. Days I wanted to bail and just go home. Adam and I often commiserated about how hard it was sometimes just to get out of bed in the morning and keep going.

"Sometimes it's a long hard slog," Adam shared with me one day.

Just like life, I thought. Some days it's all we can do to keep going.

I've given up on many things in my life. But I didn't quit the Camino. On those mornings I could barely stand another day of walking, I would turn the walk over to Source, then pray for strength and perseverance. I would try not to think about how many kilometres I had to do that day. I'd put on my boots and walk out the door and pray the spirit of the Camino would carry me to Santiago.

MEDITATION REVIEW

Do 15 minutes of breathing meditation, half an hour of Forgiveness Meditation.

JOURNAL EXERCISE

What age were you when you were most deeply wounded? Disappointed? Heartbroken? Did others harm you when you were small? Did you harm yourself with excessive compulsions, addictions or self-sabotage? Write a letter to that wounded child whom no one protected. Forgive that part of yourself. Remember what kept you going.

ACTION STEP

Leave your letter under a rock along the path or at the Cruz de Ferro. Give it to Source to forgive and release. If you are fatigued, pray for strength and perseverance. Inhale strength, exhale weariness. Keep on walking.

DAY TWENTY-EIGHT | *The Camino Is Going to Santiago, Where Are You Going?*

One afternoon while walking with my friends, Adam and Klaus, we passed a sign scrawled on a wall that read: *Camino va a Santiago. Que es su va?*

"Translation?" I asked Adam.

"The Camino is going to Santiago," Adam translated. "Where are you going?"

"Good question," I said.

"I won't know until I arrive there," Klaus said.

We spent the rest of that morning talking about where we were going in life. It was a common Camino question. My friend Sam had bravely given away all her possessions and was walking the Camino looking for a new direction. Adam had given up his robes and was walking as a way to ease himself into civilian life. Klaus was also looking for direction for his future, and love I think too. Many people I came across were at a crossroads, walking to overcome a loss or find inspiration or direction. The Camino was a kind of mid-course correction. As a Celtic Druid I met earlier explained to me, walking The Way, realigns you with your true purpose in this life. But what if we don't know what that is? In that case I like the advice my friend Sue, a former nun gave me: "When you're stuck, pray until something happens." On pilgrimage, we walk until something happens.

MEDITATION FOR
TRANSFORMING OBSTACLES

Connect with Source. As you walk, breathe deeply, scanning your body from top to bottom, looking for any areas of anxiety or tension. Is there any place that feels stuck? What feeling does it have? What shape or colour? If it is fear, silently repeat: May I be free of fear. Then ask yourself: What would destroy fear? What is the opposite of fear? Is it not faith? So now as you walk inhale faith. Exhale fear. Breathe in faith as white light. Breathe out fear as dark smoke that disappears through the soles of your feet into the earth. Go through every mental obstacle like this breathing in the antidote for whatever ails you. Here are some examples: Fear/faith, resistance/acceptance, pain/comfort, complaint/gratitude, etc. Breathe in the antidote as you walk until it neutralizes your discomfort. Then walk and breathe. Treading gently on Mother Earth.

DAY TWENTY-NINE

Once a Pilgrim, Always a Pilgrim

S ahagun is an old town named after a Roman martyr. The day I arrived I went to see the cathedral, La Peregrina, meaning Lady Pilgrim. Inside I heard laughter and as my eyes adjusted to the darkness, I recognized Adam and Jason in the church. They were flirting and joking around with the tour guide. She was tiny with dark hair and lively eyes, a serious face. Still, she was playing along.

"*Estoy tanto y loco*," Jason said, trying to practice his beginner Spanish. "*Como se dice* crazy?" He meant to say I am fat and crazy. He was wearing his ball cap backwards. Adam was courteous and translated Jason's faulty Spanish. The tour guide was charmed.

"*No usted tanto*," she corrected him. "*Usted gordo*," then she giggled. She had a girl's face but I noticed her hair was gently graying. She was no fool. She told us she had worked at the cathedral for many years.

"*Estoy peregrina, soy peregrina*," she said, sagely.

"Once a pilgrim, always a pilgrim," Adam translated.

It seemed devout and very serious on her part, but after I'd finished walking, I understood. There's something that happens when you perambulate the Camino's endless kilometres doing a spiritual practice. It's like an ambulatory retreat. After walking for weeks, you feel different about yourself, different about your fellows, different about the land and about your life. In the end you walk right out of the person you were and into a new resonance. You become a pilgrim. And once a pilgrim, always a pilgrim.

MEDITATION REVIEW

Continue to practice Meditation for Transforming Obstacles for half an hour every morning. Then walk in silence and watch your breath for 15 minutes.

JOURNAL EXERCISE

Write about your day. How was your spiritual practice today? Did you take good care of your feet, make good use of this precious human rebirth? Do you have any apologies to make? Anything you wish you had done or said differently? Anything you would like to do better tomorrow?

ACTION STEP

Give thanks for what was good. Say a prayer about what was difficult. Then let it go and sleep peacefully.

DAY THIRTY | *Kissing Samadhi*

A t one point on the Camino, my friend Sam and I climbed 800 metres straight up to one of the high points of the Camino, O'Cebreiro. After scaling the summit, over lunch Sam confessed: "I don't even know what life is for." I thought about that for a long time. What is life for? In recovery, addicts work toward a life of sane and happy usefulness. In Mahayana Buddhism, we meditate to calm our minds but also to aid other sentient beings. In therapy we learn to be more conscious of our feelings and motives and heal our past wounds in the hopes of achieving our potential and cultivating better relationships with others. I had done years of therapy and meditation, but suddenly I was tired and didn't have an answer to Sam's question.

At Radmila A Rua the old pilgrim hospital where Sam and I stayed for a day or so to rest, we ran into our pal Klaus, the German yogi. When Klaus showed up, he was glowing. He stood in front of the setting sun and rays shot out from around his head. He told us he had just kissed samadhi.

We laughed. I thought he had just had a mystical experience, as in the Buddhist experience of oneness with all, but Sam corrected me and said he had just kissed a girl.

Klaus explained that he had kissed a Hungarian girl, whose yogic name was Samadhi.

"So is your statement literal or metaphorical?" I asked.

"Both. You would know if you had kissed Samadhi." Then he wandered off in his blissful state.

Sam and I laughed. I thought kissing samadhi was a brilliant metaphor. We all want to be loved. To feel connected. To be at peace with ourselves and our world. We all want to Kiss Samadhi. Maybe that was what life was for.

THE GOD WITHIN MEDITATION

Visualize Source above your head as you walk and breathe. What are the qualities of an enlightened being? Of God? Generosity? Kindness? Compassion? Equanimity? Imagine Source sending you these qualities in the form of a joyful rainbow light. These divine qualities become a diamond that sinks into the top of your head and takes up residence in your heart. As you walk the diamond turns clockwise illuminating every corner of your being, destroying all negativity, worry, doubt, or fear. You and Source are now connected. Inhale this pure clarity and joy from Higher Consciousness. As you exhale, your heart expands, and the diamond at your heart rotates sending out love for your fellow beings. Walk like this, inhaling unconditional love in the form of radiant light, while sending out goodness and kindness with every step.

DAY THIRTY-ONE
The Lessons of the Pilgrim

I walked into Santiago with Klaus and my friend Sam. Sam could hardly walk and Klaus had to carry her knapsack on top of his own. We were delirious from walking so long. It had been a wonderful morning, walking through the gum forest, singing, chanting, and chatting. Galicia is full of lovely tall eucalyptus trees whose leaves shimmer in the wind. But the forest was long gone, we were facing a city, and walking into Santiago felt suddenly overwhelming. There was traffic, diesel fumes, streetlights, crowds and chaos. I was flooded with feelings of elation and sadness. The walk was over, but suddenly I felt I hadn't achieved anything. I was still the same imperfect soul, still prey to feeling uncomfortable in my own skin, still full of feelings bigger than I could sometimes contain. We stopped at a supermarket to get some food. The store was full of shoppers almost frantic with busyness. The sight of so many rushing people was overwhelming too. Afterwards, we sat on a busy street eating to stabilize our blood sugar levels. We began to share how we were feeling now that we were nearing our goal and the end of our journey. Everyone agreed to feeling a tad despondent.

"My teacher always says," Klaus went on, "in the end all is emptiness. You get to the end, and you see that everything is empty. That's what we're feeling-the emptiness."

I nodded. What had I hoped the Camino would do for me? I wondered. Make me perfect? Enlightened?

Over the next few days, Sam and I checked into a fabulous hotel, received our official stamped *Compostela,* or Pilgrim's Certificate, and went to mass. Wandered through the pilgrim museum. We reunited with friends for dinner. After a few days it just felt abnormal not to walk. So, we decided to walk a few days more.

MEDITATION REVIEW

Pick your favourite meditation practice and do it for 45 minutes.

JOURNAL EXERCISE

How do you feel now that you've nearly finished your month-long walk? What Camino lessons you would like to integrate into your life at home? Of all the meditations in this small book, which worked best for you? What made you feel closer to your Source? When did you experience, grace, wisdom or loving kindness? What daily spiritual practice would you like to continue practicing? What would you let go of?

ACTION STEP

Is it time to find a twelve-step group, a meditation class, a sponsor, mentor, meditation teacher or other support group? Make a promise to nourish your higher self, the Divine within. And to find like-minded friends to walk with on your life journey.

DAY THIRTY-TWO
Joy @ the End of the World

I found the last three days of walking agonizing. I slogged, it was a struggle. The road between Santiago and Finisterre on the coast was hilly and wild. We had to walk long distances between alburgues and towns. It was mid-July and very hot. On the last morning, before Finisterre, Sam and I climbed and climbed. We were getting close to the end, every moment felt sacred, every sight precious. We had done ten kilometres in a pinch that morning, but still we climbed.

Finally, giddy with fatigue we crested a peak where there was an enormous cross. We conquered the ridge and there, finally, was the Atlantic Ocean below, nothing but water stretching to the horizon.

"Fins terre," Sam said. We had reached the end of the world. Soon there would be no more walking. I felt joy, relief, sadness, sorrow, pride. We still had to descend but that one glimpse of ocean carried me for hours. When we got to the outskirts of town, Sam felt ill and climbed into her sleeping bag to rest while I went to a small café to watch the sea. There were families on holiday, children rushed around in their bathing suits or built fortresses in the sand. After seven weeks of slogging often through wind and rain, we were now suddenly at a seaside resort in summer, a place of fun and rest.

What was all this walking for? As I sat there, sipping a cold drink, dolphins suddenly appeared in the surf. They leapt into the air, the sun glinting off their shiny metal-coloured hides. I stood in awe. They cavorted in the surf for no other reason than joy. They gave it their all, leapt for the sky then plunged back into the water, in turns. I thought that's it, that's my answer: *Follow your joy.* I was right back at the beginning. Follow the arrows. That was the point. Joy. Bliss. Happiness.

LOVING KINDNESS FOR ALL MEDITATION

Walk in silence. Head in the sky, feet touching the earth. Watch your breath for a few moments. Now visualize Source above your head, emanating a joyful white light that enters your crown chakra. Think of all those good qualities Source embodies for you: Goodness, compassion, wisdom, forgiveness, hope, faith, grace, courage, generosity, and discipline. List them. Feel those qualities entering you in the form of white light. The sunlight of the spirit fills every corner of your body. If any negativity remains, have it leave through your feet in the form of dark smoke until the transmission is complete. Now you and Higher Consciousness are one. You are the Source. Greet everything and everyone that crosses your path, a stone, a yellow arrow, a fellow pilgrim with the sacred wish: *May you be free of suffering, may you be at peace.* See that all these sentient beings also have Buddha nature, Christ consciousness, Diamond Mind. Walk like this, sending out kindness, love and joy from your heart with every step.

EPILOGUE | *The End is Only The Beginning*

My re-entry into society was the bumpiest imaginable. I walked all the way to Finisterre, then celebrated my seven-week sobriety with warm champagne. It was only then that I admitted I was an alcoholic, but now I had to start all over again. I promptly got lost in a fog, then got on a bus the next morning to go to the airport. In London, I felt traumatized by the busyness of Heathrow airport. I plummeted into post-Camino blues. I share all this so that you will never suffer the same. The Camino is a retreat, and re-entry into the modern world needs to be gentle as I learned the hard way. Celebrate your magnificent accomplishment, but treat yourself like you would a newborn, with tenderness, with care.

I have a quote in my office that goes like this: "Never regret, if it's good, it's wonderful, if it's bad, it's experience." The good bad news was, I was so nostalgic for the Camino I went to a pilgrim gathering soon after I arrived home, at a beautiful seaside town. They weren't my Camino tribe whom I missed terribly, but they understood the lure of the road. I fell in love with that quaint village on Lake Huron, and I went there every summer on holiday for years. It turned out to be another gift from the Camino. At the gathering someone shared: "The real Camino begins at home."

One month later, I got sober for good. Fingers crossed.

I didn't understand this at first, but gradually the idea began to sink in. On the road we learn so much about ourselves, about our minds, our core issues, and our essential life themes. Big stuff that takes time to truly assimilate. The real work is integrating the lessons of the walk, allowing them to change our lives for the better. I still feel like I'm learning the lessons of the Camino, which is why I wrote this little book. So that I would remember what The Way taught me. Also, so that I could remind myself daily that life is a Camino, a great walk, a sacred journey, to be enjoyed and shared with others.

BASIC BREATHING MEDITATION

Go back to the beginning. Every day we begin anew with beginner's mind. While you walk pay attention to your breath. Feel the air as it enters your nostrils. Notice how wondrous it is just to breathe deeply. How strange that something so simple, could give so much happiness. Walk while watching your breath for five minutes.

ACTION STEP

Do an act of selfless service. You can volunteer to become a *hospitalero* or host on the Camino. Or volunteer for something at home. Help a neighbour, listen to a troubled friend, visit someone who is sick. No one need thank you for this. This is karma yoga. *Seva.* Service. This is part of giving back what you've been given. Continue to go mindful walking, while connecting with Higher Power and cultivating the Source within. Peace be with you. *Soha.* Amen.

ACKNOWLEDGEMENTS

Most of the wisdom included here was inspired by my meditation teachers, mentors, psychotherapists, and sponsors. I would like to thank them for their kindness and generosity: Buddhist teachers—Lama Thubten Yeshe, Lama Zopa Rinpoche, and Dekyi-Lee Oldershaw of Lama Yeshe Ling; the Venerable Ayang Rinpoche, Insight Meditation Teacher Norman Feldman, and Jivasu of Naturality Meditation School, in Hamilton, Ontario; as well as my spiritually-inclined therapists Susan Wood and Jean Rankin, sponsors and friends Pat and Sue, not to mention my life coach, Shelley Hannah and writing coach, Barbara Turner-Vesselago. Thank you one and all. A special thanks to my soul friends who walked The Way with me in Spain. You made the journey funny and unforgettable.

ABOUT THE AUTHOR

Kelly Watt is an award-winning author and poet. She has published two books, the novel *Mad Dog*, (2001/2019) and the mini book, *Camino Meditations* (2013). In 2019, her essay, *The Road for Conquering*, was included in *Nowhere Magazine's* best of travel writing, and won an honorary mention at gritLIT, the Hamilton Readers and Writers Festival. She began studying Tibetan Buddhism at the age of 18 in Nepal and has completed three pilgrimages, in India, Mexico and Spain. Kelly is also an EFT International practitioner, and certified meditation teacher with the Naturality School, of Hamilton, Ontario (2015.)